EVIDENCE OF GOD

EVIDENCE OF GOD

A Final Resolution of Meaning

Mercury Jones

iUniverse, Inc.
New York Lincoln Shanghai

Evidence of God
A Final Resolution of Meaning

Copyright © 2008 by Mercury Jones

iUniverse books may be ordered through booksellers or by contacting:

iUniverse
2021 Pine Lake Road, Suite 100
Lincoln, NE 68512
www.iuniverse.com
1-800-Authors (1-800-288-4677)

ISBN: 978-0-595-48644-1 (pbk)
ISBN: 978-0-595-60739-6 (ebk)

Printed in the United States of America

"The fear of God is the beginning of knowledge; but fools despise wisdom and instruction."

Proverbs 1:7

Contents

Acknowledgments

This work was made possible through the generous conversations that have taking place on the path in which, I believe, was meant for me—that which has given me meaning. Not only those, but them that came before them and those that will surely come after. There have been too many contributors to personally name but their thoughts, ideas and fingerprints are all over this work.

Upon completion of this book, in me I feel there is none. By that, I mean to say that now I only seem to know the next step to take. It appears to follow my next question, my next thought of course. Each step just another continual in a line of steps that is my path—a path that seems to be lead by my understanding: and that understanding lead by not me.

I'd also like to point out one fact that kept reappearing and making it known unto me. The fact that remains constant throughout is that at the end of every table, at the end of every supper, every trail is God. No matter what pretense man may have about true authority and true power, it is self evident that man remains powerless in a world of one power. So it is with a humility that far exceeds any glory that I, myself, might try to obtain that I make known whom is truly responsible for this book. He, who has breathed life and understanding into me that we all might glorify the one and only true God and His Son Jesus Christ.

To this end, this book comes forth.

Introduction

This book is just that, a book. It is meant to give to the reader, a sense of meanings and of knowledge applied, as it relates to man and the relationship of objects, activity and phenomenon that make up his world. These relationships are self evident and are justified in their practice and offers, one, the means as to a way to think and to think more, better. This book will also examine the dichotomy of language and its presuppositions. This book hopes to expose the true nature of knowledge and language. This is this books sense and purpose; a mere reflection of a perspective.

CLOSETS

CHAPTER 1

To know something is to know what it is not

A. How do I distinguish up? How do I distinguish down?

1. If there exist a plain that has no value (Draw horizontal line) and is neutral to all relationships, then the difference from the neutral point represents its alternatives, up, down, beside or some variation of the three. Anything above or higher than the neutral would represent up or above. As would be the case of anything lower than the neutral would represent down or below. Then the alternatives become neutrals creating an existing body of knowledge

2. Could the same be said for good and bad? Is there a neutral with good and bad as its alternatives? Is your existence a neutral?

D. Knowing cause I know: Recognizing one thing is a declaration of knowing what it is not. If two things are identical, you know one exist independent of the other. (You can see that) You recognizing one declares it is not the other. You can't get to two counting without one.

E. Agreement is knowing: I know black because there is agreement of what black is. (We have agreed that Black represents a color, a people, a consciousness in our common reality.)

F. Internal Properties and External Structure make up the thing to know

1. Totalities or speaking in general can be nonsensical if the thing or object being spoken of is not known totally.

2. What is in the box?

3. You don't know what is in the box until you look inside of it. If you don't know the entirety of the box, can you talk sense about its entirety? To talk about the totality of the box, I would have to know its internal properties and its external structure.

4. Can I talk sense about the totality of the world?

5. If the entirety is unknown, then there exists a limit to what can be said but not thought.

6. Do we know every person in the world? Then what can be said about those people? Can I say, people do silly things and convey true meaning? What people am I commenting on? Is the statement more misleading than accurate? Will it lead to more questions or have I made crystal clear the true meaning of my thought?

Practicality Exercise (1)

1. Create a not list of yourself. Be truthful and as accurate as possible. Listed below is an example of a not list.

1. Not a murderer
2. Not an electrician
3. Not white
4. Not Jewish
5. Not female
6. Not overweight
7. Not Rich
8. Not born in California

Give as much detail as you can. It will help develop and pinpoint who you see yourself as and how you see yourself.

2. Determine what your Neutral is. Answer the question: What is the base essence of my existence? What is my nature or what appears to be natural to me in the capacity of relationships?

1. Good relationship: Equal amount of love, unconditional, growth, happiness
2. Neutral Relationship: Allowed to be me, do whatever want, my world, my existence
3. Bad relationship: One sided, stagnant, miserable

3. Look Inside Your Box and Know Your Properties: Create a list of your internal properties. Below is a short example.

1. Empathy
2. Generous
3. Hatefulness
4. Jealousy
5. Compassionate
6. Forgiveness

G. The Use of a Thing is its Knowing

1. I know a cup because of its function. It holds material and can be used for immediate access to that material.

2. If a thing is able to be used as the thing it represents, then it is by its use, a kind of or a type of the thing.

3. A cup has a purpose and by its use fulfills that purpose.

4. A thing used to fulfill the same purpose is by its use a kind of or type of the thing.

5. Is a clock a clock because it tells time? What about a watch? Would they both cease from being the things they are if their purpose were different? What if the clock was broken, would it still be a clock?

H. My Use of the Thing is determined by Its Knowing

1. Can I know I can write a symphony until I write it? Can I know how to ride a bike until I actually ride it? I may think it is possible but not until I do it is my knowing of it proved.

2. If the use of the thing is knowing, is not using not knowing?

3. I cannot know the thing I do not know until I know it. What then do I really know? Is it what I have done?

4. Proof is in the observable.

I. Proof and Verification: Proof lies in what I can prove

1. Tests are proof of knowledge and stands as examples or symbols of proof itself.

2. How can one know if the answer is known to the question: 1 + 1, unless the problem is solved.

3. How do you prove the money is in the safe? You have to physically be present in or at the safe, to observe it to be positive it is in there.

4. Outside proof lays Science, Hope, Faith and Speculation.

A. Proof of God outside of nature is faith.

B. Proof of the future is speculation (Gambling, Stocks)

C. Proof of the past is science. .

D. If observation of the event or object is proof, then the past has no proof outside of those who have observed it. Science only gives evidence of the proof that is hoped for.

E. Prove that you were here yesterday. Can you prove that? An erect building only proves that the erect building exist only at the moment you observe it. It must be silent on everything else.

Practicality Exercise (2)

1. To know the list of the use of a thing: List your purpose for your use. For what purpose does your make up avail? Below is a sample list.

1. Caregiver
2. Comforter
3. Protagonist
4. Provider
5. Christian
6. Founder

2. Make a list of things you know; things you've known to do. Be specific. Below is a sample list.

1. Writer
2. Husband
3. Ex-husband
4. Cameraman
5. Rent payer
6. Jerk

CHAPTER 2

Identities and Symbols

A. A Thing is itself and is identified as itself and nothing else and therefore cannot be something else singularly.

B. A Thing is distinguishable from another Thing with similar properties because they are separate. No two things can have all the same properties because that would make them one.

C. How do you tell twins apart? They have similar qualities but not all are the same. One stands out that is observable: the separate quality.

D. Each Thing Stands Independent of the other Thing

    1. Is the world a collection of things/objects? Is man just another thing in the collection?

    2. Man is in relationship with the other objects in the world.

E. Other Things make up Other Things, but it is all relational

    1. A watch is made up of other parts. A sentence is made up of parts. A sentence is part of a paragraph and so on …

    2. Natural things exist without our intervention while non-natural things exist because of our intervention.

3. The things that make up the thing to know, is not the thing itself, but together make up the thing to know.

A. No one player is a team. The collection is the team.

B. Is a king his kingdom? Does he need those to rule over?

4. The actions of the thing may take on characteristics of the thing, but may never be the thing.

A. Events or activity don't make an object.

B. One player playing is not the team in play.

C. A king by himself is no kingdom

F. One Thing may stand in place for the other thing but may never be the thing it is standing in for.

1. A symbol is a representation of the actual thing.

2. The word "rock" stands in place for the object rock in my sentence: The rock is on the ground. So, the word "ground" stands in place for the object, earth or dirt, in reality.

3. A symbol may have similar properties to the thing it represents but may never be the actual object.

A. If you have DNA of a person, is it the actual person?

B. If you cloned that DNA, would it be the actual person you took the DNA from or would it be an identical clone (separate) of the person you took the DNA from?

C. Am I my soul, if "I" is a symbol and my soul is a symbol? It appears that "I" cannot be both.

G. A Symbol may be represented by another Symbol.

1. Sign language is a symbol for the spoken word, as words, themselves, are mere representation of the actual reality they stand in for.

2. The symbol for the word chair in sign language is symbol of the word chair in spoken or written language is a symbol for the actual chair itself.

3. If there be an infinite possibility of the symbols, then is there an infinite possibility of expression, in (as) language, in math, in art?

4. If words be symbols of reality, then are sentences expressions of reality? And if reality is speaking, then its sentences should correspond to that reality, right? They should, as close as possible, reflect the truest reality possible.

5. "Is" and "On" expresses the relationship of the pen and the table in the sentence: The pen is on the table.

6. Logic shows, it does not explain.

7. The pen and the table are both showing using, "Is" and "On"

8. The logic takes on object form because it has a purpose to fulfill.

I. Symbols may stand in for Activity or Phenomenon.

1. Gravity is a word that represents an Activity or Phenomenon. It is not like a full object or thing but in fact is a kind of a relational object, in that it needs other objects to be observed.

2. A concept may take on the characteristics of an object but may never be an object independent of other objects.

3. Racism may appear to be an object, independent of other objects, but it needs other objects to be observed.

4. Is good an Activity or Phenomenon?

Practicality Exercise (3).

1. Combine list (3) three and (5) five on the left side of the page and combine list (1) one and (4) four on the right side of the page. The relation will give you the ability to see yourself more clearly.

Internal Properties (3) Not List (1)

$X * n/y -X/X * n$

Know List (5) Possibilities (4)

2. The left side of the page is your box: the totality of your box. The right side gives you the impression of why the left side is as the left side. One may explain the other—a symbol. Can one be substituted for another? How? In the analysis of your life, can these symbols help you understand? See how one can stand in for the other.

CHAPTER 3

Value

A Value is a Property of a Thing

A. If a value is a property of a thing and not the thing itself, then wet, the value, is only tied to the thing and is not the thing itself. Therefore, wet must have an object to tie to and can never be an object independent.

B. Is good a value?

C. If wet is tied to an object and is represented as an alternative to its neutral, then is wet possible for any object? What about water?

D. There exist Natural Values and Moral values. Natural Values stand outside the person while Moral Values stand within the person. Good is moral value. What is wet? Confusion arises from these two misuses.

E. Natural values may be tied to any object except the object from which it derives its natural state. Water can many other things but never wet.

F. Moral Values stand inside the person but exist without. Human decency exist whether we acknowledge it or not, but good is tied to an object.

G. Values ought to naturally speak in public because privately they speak only to those privy. Natural values speak about the world while moral values talks about us.

H. We are not the world. We are a part of it.

I. The values that stand inside of us speak from our pulpits.

J. If we are talking about the world, then we should speak naturally.

CHAPTER 4

Wisdom

Applied Knowledge is True Understanding

A. Wisdom is the Proof of Understanding

1. Proof exists: Observable through the senses.

2. I put a pen on the table. What proof do you have that the pen is on the table? The pen itself existing as you see it or touch it in a reality that is common to us all. It exists and is immediately available through the senses as a proof test of reality. "Pinch me."

3. Evidence and Proof are separate. They both are themselves and as words, represent different phenomenon in reality.

4. What proof can we have of the past? Can we go back to the past and observe it? Does proof exist only in the moment?

5. What does the existence of a building prove? Does it prove the past or only the immediate?

6. Can I prove I wasn't the murderer if my DNA was left behind at the crime scene or does the proof lay against the DNA, which is just evidence?

7. The existence of the DNA at the crime scene is only proof the DNA was found there. It was observed there. The question still remains, how it got there. Is there any proof of how it got there?

8. Am I my DNA or is my DNA, my DNA, a representative for me? If I grow the DNA I found at the crime scene into a complete human, would it be the same exact person the original DNA came from?

9. Does Science prove proof? Scientists come back to reality when proving there theories.

10. If proof exist only in the immediate and is observable through the senses, then is the activity of understanding wisdom?

11. Is teaching proof of my understanding? I have to show to teach.

12. The Wisdom of this book is in its activity.

LIGHT SWITCHES

CHAPTER 5

Self

Know Thy Soul

A. The "who" to know stands separate from the know of I. To know me, is to know what I am not.

B. If the theory of identity is clear, then am I my soul? Are the soul and I one or does the soul exists independent of I? So the who to know is the soul not I or me. So the question: Am I my soul, makes sense in the same sense that I am not my soul, they are separate. Know the soul.

C. The internal soul and the external soul are the things to know.

D. The internal soul has properties that make up the thing to know. Those internal properties are not the soul, they are themselves. My soul then stands neutral to its alternatives.

E. What is the neutral of my internal soul separate from its alternatives? Is to exist the neutral of the internal/external soul?

F. The external of my soul is not I. "I" is itself. The external of the soul is its structure, its form.

G. The make up of the internal properties form the external soul.

H. To know the external form is to know the make up of the internal properties.

I. To know the use of the soul is to know the soul.

1. I and me are symbols used to stand in for the soul. I is me and self in use and are themselves not the soul.

2. If language reflects reality, then the use of the symbols for the soul is as stand-ins.

3. Therefore, I, me and self refer to the internal soul and its make up that forms its external form.

4. Who are I, me and self? They are not the soul. They are I, me and self.

5. If my soul is inside the box, then the box is itself. What is the box?

6. The box reflects the soul as language shadows reality. Therefore, like language, the box may be misleading as to the reality of the actual soul.

7. I and the box represent the soul but are not the soul, therefore they can themselves be not used as the actual soul, only as stand-ins for the soul. The soul itself, as well, can stand in for itself, like now.

8. The beginning and end of my soul will be the beginning and end of me in use.

9. I has life but the soul affords it.

10. Without the soul, I has no life.

11. Whatever I do, my soul is responsible for it.

12. Life begins with the soul.

13. Good and mercy may make up the soul.

14. Seeing the properties of my soul is seeing my soul.

15. Good clings to the soul and could be replaced at any time.

16. The picture of the soul is it alternatives.

17. I possess some of the characteristics of the soul.

18. If you have me, you don't have my soul.

19. I was born, but my soul existed before.

20. My body stands in for my body and is not my soul.

21. If I stands in for my soul, can it stand in for my body too?

22. I needs to distinguish who I stands in for when I speaks.

23. Matthew 10:28

24. I owns nothing, my soul belongs to God.

CHAPTER 6

Others

(Relations)

A. To know others is to know their internal properties and external form.

1. The external form is observable, then provable. Can I know your hair color? Can the internal properties be proved?

2. Can I know your thoughts, your sensations independent of your communicating them to me?

3. What I can know is what can be known to me. What can be known to me can only be known from me unless we can agree upon what known means outside of me.

A. If I can lift 190 lbs. and no more, then is everything that weights over 190 lbs. weight the same?

B. Can I possible know how much 2000 lbs weight? We can agree that it is heavy and beyond our known physical capacity to lift, therefore unknowable.

B. To know others use is to know others

1. The relation of A to B is the sum, "we". If A to B were A no relation B, then we would cease to exist.

2. If "we" is a combination, then is it a combination of combinations?

    A. If A can lift 100 lbs. and B can lift 100 lbs., together can they lift 200 lbs.?

    B. If A has a pain and B has a pain, is pain increased when they come together?

    C. Combinations can combine and increase in natural value but not in moral value.

        1. My pain may be felt by you once you can identify with it.

        2. My love and your love may increase the amount of love we do, but not the amount of love we have.

C. The sum of two numbers is the whole of one.

    1. In math, we stands in the middle of you and I. $1 + 1 = 2$

    2. "We" is a compromise of you and I together.

    3. If an object may be made up of other objects (complex), then we may stand in for an object.

    4. The we that represents I, consist of objects independent of I. If I, minus an object previous, exist, then is I the same as before or is I a different I because I has new constituent parts; a new form? The moment I's internal properties change, the relations of the properties change too, forcing the structure to change.

    5. A new creature consists of a new structure.

    6. Me and You are not we. We may stand in for us, those and ours.

    7. We see things different from I, me and you. They are all four different perspectives.

    8. Teamwork is used by we, while I likes to work alone.

    9. We fought wars for my freedom.

    10. God created I, made we, willed I so that we all might be one.

    11. I exist only on earth; we will make it to Heaven.

    12. Adding more I's to we, adds more relationships.

13. The moment the I's have it, we may be used.

14. If I don't communicate with you, we may never be.

15. We generalize because we think we have all the information.

16. I is greater than we in selfishness.

17. If we agree what pain is, then I can identify it.

CHAPTER 7

The World

The world represents that which exists as a collection of objects and is comprised of everything that it is comprised of to know.

1. Is the list of objects in the world all there is to know about the world?

2. The objects in the world stand in relation to each other and represent facts that exist about our common reality.

3. These facts are the basis of our understanding, such as Science, Mathematics, Philosophy, etc. It is a fact that light, which is a wave and a particle, contains certain chemicals compounds in it is the basis of how astronomers calculate what chemicals exist off Earth. The light from stars and other cosmological phenomenon are composed of things or objects that are themselves and can be exercised to reveal further facts about that same common reality.

4. These facts about the relations of the objects in our world comprise a list of facts in a sense. This list of facts is our world in a sense. They allow for understanding, which allows to more understanding, which allows for more … Allowing for growth or an illusion of growth in the body of knowledge.

5. The list of facts stand in conjunction with the list of non-fact fact: about the relations of the objects in our world. This is, in a sense, a non-fact facts list that also is representative of our common reality.

6. Every object in the world is relative to what is in relation with.

A. Perspective is only a way to see the object.

B. To know the full collection and its relationships is to know what the world represents.

What these sentences attempts to establish is the nature between words and objects, words and activity, and words and the natural phenomenon they stand in to represent. These sentences also look to establish the meaninglessness of words, even when these words are being used to communicate. In that, the relationships of the aforementioned, quite possible, could stand as the basis for realizing a truer meaning in the thoughts that are being expressed using any form of language.

Before we begin, let's establish a fact that may aid us in our journey through these ideas. First we should be aware that words and language are two separate entities. They both, then, require two separate functions and two separate purposes.

We use words within language. Language is a system used by those engaged in communicating. The system or the language's structure is what will determine the next step in the process. The next step in understanding or using a language is to know its constituent parts. And for the English language and many other languages, words are one of the constituent parts. Other entities that are used by language or make up its parts are punctuations such as periods and commas and definitions (agreements). They along with words, make up some of the things to know. For example, the word "the" may be the most used word in the English language. In its use, it seems to have a specific function and a specific purpose. That purpose and function are easily seen by the structure of the English language; it's grammatical code. The function of the word 'the' in language is to help establish thought, while the purpose of the word is to represent some part of the thought within the expression. Yet the structure or code of the English language can not define the words used by it. It merely provides a place for them. The grammatical code realized in English stands separate from the words used in it. Each has its own separate function and purpose.

Let's take a closer look. What does the word "chair" appear to mean? Most people would answer the question the same way. They would merely try to repeat Webster's chronicled rendition of meaning. If that is the case, then what does the word chair represent? Does the word "chair" mean what it is standing in for? Is definition meaning? What if there were a table and a chair presently before us and I say to you, "That chair is shaky." What would the word chair appear to mean in this sentence? Would the word chair in this sentence mean its definition or the specific object? Is meaning specific?

Is it possible for meaning be two things? If a thing is itself and only itself, can meaning be itself and something else? Can meaning be function and purpose both? If that is the case, what then is purpose or function, are they both meaning? If they are both meaning, then why are they both necessary? So when we ask, what is the function of words in language are we asking, what is the meaning of words in language? If that is so, what is the purpose of words in language? Is it meaning? This leads to a un-escapable conclusion that meaning can not be both function and purpose.

If we accept meaning existing as a definition, then does meaning exist before the definition or after the definition? If meaning is present before the definition, then meaning is not the definition. If meaning exists after the definition, then meaning would appear to be agreement. If meaning is agreement then is disagreement non-meaning? And does the meaning change with the definition? For instance, the word "wave", does it mean the same thing in different contexts? Is a wave, a wave? What is the correct definition of wave? Is it the rhythmic pattern observed in nature or is it the activity that is engaged in when one is exiting? If your answer is both then meaning is not a definition. It is existence. The definition only tries to explain or define what is being observed. A more appropriate sentence might clarify what is truly trying to be expressed: It would appear, we try to make meaning out of what is observed when meaning is what is being observed. If meaning of "chair" is an actual object, then what meaning does a definition have? Can a definition have meaning? If meaning can not be a definition, then a words meaning appears to be the object, activity or phenomenon.

A word appears to have a distinct meaning before it is being used in a sentence. Yet once combined together in certain and distinct ways with other words, the set and defined word appears to morph, to evolve into a new creation—similar but separate. Although, the new definition and the old definition appear to have similar characteristics tied to them, but the distinct difference is apparent. That is the case or they would be one. Our beloved institution, the dictionary, makes clear this concept when it numbers definitions of the same word. Webster has declared one not to be the other.

In its rarest form, a word may seem definite in meaning. Tree. Rock. Man—all actual objects we can observe. Proof of them exists. But if you take a closer look at the words being used as you communicate, it becomes apparently obvious that some words when attached to other words, can begin to take on new and different connotation; multiple meanings in a sense, as in the case of the propositions: "Tree of good and evil" or "Book of life". Have there existed objects that we can directly identify and call it a tree of good and evil or a book that we call the book of life? Or do these exist as multiple meaning propositions, meant to express a deeper or richer sense within the thought? If that is the case, it, then falls to the one receiving the conveyed thought to interpret these propositions correctly to understand the true idea being expressed or at least, be able to speculate on it.

The word once combined with other words, and having a new and distinct definition, either in conjunction with other words or alone, seems to offer a more detailed and expansive thought. What is this phenomenon? Is the word actually changing its meaning or is the word simple being tied to a different object, activity, or phenomenon? Different from the original object, activity or phenomenon it was originally standing in for? If it is entirely different then wouldn't that make it separate and distinct on its own. Well, if that is true, then in fact, the word has morph, evolved or changed, or at least, for what it is standing in for. But that fact does not change the other fact that the word has not changed its function.

Do words have real meaning? If a word is a symbol, purposed to represent within the thought, fixed in function within the language, and is not the actual thing it represents and stands separate from that thing totally, then does the symbol have any actual meaning? Can the symbol stand on its own and still have function or purpose within a language? What function would a symbol serve in a language if that word wasn't tied to anything? Can "X" be just "X" and still mean something within any structure? As proof, Mathematics exist an example. If that is not the case, what would it be standing in for, itself? Is a word an object, activity or phenomenon that is in need of a stand in itself? Where is the word in reality? Is the word in reality, the object, activity or phenomenon or is it the word displayed in reality? If it is the display of the word which is the word in reality, then the display of the word must exist in reality before the word not in reality. Does this occur? If not, then it is the object, activity or phenomenon, then that gives the word its meaning.

So what exactly is meaning? If function and purpose are themselves, can meaning be existence or can meaning be representation? In fact, meaning has to be itself. So what do we mean when we say, what is the meaning? Since we are not asking what is the purpose or function of it, are we simple asking if it is itself? It is a minor error on our behalf which comes from our misunderstanding of the use of words within language. If we are interested in knowing, we should be asking, what is it standing in for? Although it is abundantly clear that function and purpose are central to understanding, identifying the phenomenon or establishing what a word is referencing, even within its own context, appears to be the necessary key to unlocking any thought.

The purpose for the word is to stand in: to symbolize. What it is symbolizing stands within its own context. The function of the word is to be used within the language by language, itself and its participants or those engaged in its use. The representation, the word or what it is symbolizes is based in reality. What a word seems to means is itself, if it could. Can it—only if it observable. Then that would make it reality, right? The purpose and function are the fundamental constants to a language. The variable appears to be the symbol, who is standing in for whom.

Then a words meaning is no meaning. Whatever it is representing—whatever it is tied to or standing in for is separate from the word itself. If that is the case, then the words meaning is the word itself, not the object, activity or phenomenon it is tied to, if it could. The word itself appears to have only purpose and function—hollow shells. Meaning seems to be tied to it, in the sense of meaning is able to be observed.

Words seem to be necessary only if it is tied to an object, activity or some type of phenomenon. If there exists no language would words still be necessary? What would the word, "chair" be tied to? The word would be tied to nothing, because the word "chair" would not exist—no language. So what purpose or function would nothing have? Truth may be the thought of or the idea of a wireless phone may have existed before 1980. But if someone said the word cell phone in 1980, would anyone know the meaning of the word outside of the user of the word who is trying to describe the thought of a wireless phone? Wouldn't wireless phone be more recognizable?

Take into account the matter of Adam naming the host set before him by God in the bible. The objects are brought before Adam and he gives the names. It appears these that are to be named exist before the name is given and already had specific function and purpose. Therefore, were these before they were named, having meaning before they were named? It appears meaning was with the object not the name which came after. It seems as if names or words, according to the bible, are purposeful for language. A reason: God would have Adam name the beast, if not only to reference which beast he would be referring to when speaking of a particular beast.

Words or symbols, then, would appear to exist only as points of reference. Things used to mark out reality. Though, they are used to mark out reality, they, too can be a part of that reality they are marking out. Such as images, signs, any object, any type of distinguishable form we can agree on can function as language. And any distinguishable form we can agree on can also be used as the symbols, within that language to communicate. That being stated, and with the meaning of meaning established as to be; to exist, then it would appear that symbols, which mean to stand in for things in reality, have no meaning. Since meaning means to be and symbols stand in for things that be, then they themselves are not by their nature or function and purpose things that be. Even, if a symbol is observable, it, by its fundamental constants, cannot mean itself. Therefore, the conclusion appears to be that words, which are symbols, have no meaning, even if we agree they do.

Here is the thought pattern again for meaning in reality: (The be in meaning)

What does word mean?
Symbol.
What does symbol mean?
Representative.
What does Representative mean?
Stand In?
What does Stand in mean?
Meant to be object, activity, or phenomenon it represents.
Object, Activity, Phenomenon mean? Mean themselves; are the things that be.
Symbol only stands in for reality, not reality for symbol, even if symbol is reality.
Reality still itself, separate from symbol being used as language.

Agreement on definitions sets words up to be used by languages for communication. Though communication mandates agreement, total agreement need not be a predecessor of communication; in the sense that limited agreement may stand as the foundation entirely in order for communications to begin. The complete symbol set used within that structure can have later agreement. The moment we agree on the form of our language: words, pictures, sign language, we may begin to communicate. The confusion arises only with interpretation of the forms.

For instance, the proposition: Where would I be without my dogs ...

What is being said? Am I asking a question or making a statement? It is unclear as of yet. Taking a closer look, each word seems to be tied to specific objects, activity or phenomenon. Do the words paint a picture-able picture? Can you imagine the objects being referenced? Chances are you can. But in fact, your interpretation of the sentence may be completely separate from what is actually trying to be expressed. "Where", quite possibly, could be a spatial location or a rhetorical one? "I", may be referencing a wider group than the "I" commonly agreed upon. In some circles, "I" may be a name, hence leading you away from the most accepted definition. And the possibilities for, my dogs are numerous. Are you sure you have the true sense of what is said?

A word may, in fact, have several meanings tied to it. That same word may be expressed several different ways. The word has meaning tied to it and stands separate from the activity or object and appears to remain an empty shell: void of meaning—any true existence capacity. Even if the word is written, the capacity for it to exist outside of what is trying to represent falls short. Again, what would it be saying if the definition pointed to itself?

With these agreements, we form horizontal lists of facts and non-facts about particular objects and relationships of objects. These lists establish the base of our understanding; our body of knowledge.

For example:

1. There exist a tree, a hill and a bird.

2. The bird is in the tree.

3. The tree is on the hill.

4. The bird is in the tree on the hill.

5. A tree has a blue bird in it.

6. A blue bird is in the tree.

7. A tree on the hill has a blue bird in it.

8. A green hill and a blue bird exist.

9. A tree sits on a green hill and has a blue bird in it.

10. A blue bird sits on a tree on a green hill that has a brown tree on it.

11. A green hill has a brown tree on it.

12. A brown tree sits on a green hill.

13. A blue bird, a brown tree, and a green hill exist.

14. A brown tree has a blue bird in it and its sits on a green hill.

15. A green hill has a blue bird in the brown tree on it.

What do these sentences all have in common? They all represent a possible world; a world in which we can see, even though it may not exist. You are able to see this world because these sentences describe things and objects we know.

We know these things from their actual existence. We can observe these things; proof exists of them. We know a tree, a hill and a bird, if not personally, then through some form of second hand experience. This type of non-personal observation takes place extended from you but you believe it to be true, such as videotape, book, or some other form of recorded expressive medium. Therefore, the picture these sentences are trying to portray is picture-able to you.

Even though our world exists independent of language, in most cases, it is representative of what actually exist. The truth of the bird existing in the tree is a fact. It appears true. Truth seems to exist here at this moment about the bird, its existence and its properties. The fact that there is a tree on the hill represents another fact. These facts are facts because of the existence of the actual objects in a reality and recreating the image in your mind is not difficult.

Each word in each sentence is a part of reality in some sense and combined together with other words, build or paint a picture of a possible reality. In sentence (2) two and (3) three, there exist two facts. The two facts are a bird in a tree and a tree on a hill. These two facts are again represented in sentence (4) four with the bird in the tree on the hill. Sentence four represents another fact. The existence of the two facts together created another separate fact. The three facts stand side by side because they are equals in the world of facts—as does all other facts. The list that is created is horizontal list.

Fact 1—Fact 2—Fact 3—Fact 4—Fact 5 …

In this world we created of three objects, the possibilities for more configurations seem endless: so is the number of facts or truisms about our common reality—possible pictures. Take a look at sentence (5) five. Does it portray the same picture as its predecessors? Is there a blue bird in sentences (2, 3, 4) two, three or four? Not until sentence (5) five does a blue bird seem to appear. In fact, this bird may be a completely different bird from the bird in the previous sentences.

The other part of the list that is created is a non-facts list: a list of the opposite of the facts. For every truth, there exists its counter part, the lie or the non-truth. So every truth that makes it possible for a fact, it also makes possible the non-fact. If an orange is orange then it is not pink. The truth of it not being pink is a fact itself. It is also strung along up with the rest of the facts that make up our common understanding.

What I am pointing out is that the value of a fact seems to be one. And each fact has the same value, no more, no less. In the same way, the other words that don't necessarily correspond to objects in the sentences correspond to phenomenon that is trying to be conveyed.

If the bird is in the tree and the bird and the tree exist, then where are "is" and "in" in reality? If language is a mere reflection of what is, then these words must correspond to something, right? Can "Is" and "In" exist as the logic of the object?

This logic expresses the relation of the objects as they exist in a reality. "Is" corresponds to the existence or equal value of an object while "in" refers to the direct relation of two or more objects, actual or logical. In essence, "is" and "in" are only pointing, showing through the sentence what can be seen in reality.

Other words we use, we assign meaning to by defining it by the activity, such as when a person puts toothpaste on a toothbrush and begins to use it. We assign the word, brushing to describe that activity. We assign a word for the food we eat in the morning, breakfast. Then there are several terms used to define procreation: sex, making love, rape; all representative and viable candidates for when the sperm and the egg meet.

How then can language be truly understood? Any language, all languages seem to have one thing in common; the expression, the idea, the message that is trying to be conveyed. And the simplest way it seems to interpret any message is to take a closer look at the symbols being used and see how they are being used to ascertain a clearer understanding. Understanding, unlike facts may exist outside of language.

Is understanding in language meaning in reality? The words one may use to convey a thought are not necessarily the objects being spoke of for which the word was originally assigned to in that language. In some instances, the original defined object, activity or phenomenon may lend credibility to or offer a deeper sense to the understanding of the some what new expression: as in relating to a property or characteristic of the original object or activity.

Words appear to be tools. Tools to be used by those engaged in communicating. Depending on the context, the understandings of words change, vary, and oscillate. They all seem to be interchangeable at any moment with a common agreement. If that is the case, then it seems as if words truly are meaningless, incapable of being: it's the meaning the words are assigned to that have all the value.

Therefore, communications seems to stand as the activity engaged in when expression is the goal and that it is the means to use to explore what is to be determined. Any activity, any type of movement, any configuring, any distinguishing of form of any sort, may stand as a language and words to be used by those engaged in, in the expressing of expression.

CHAPTER 8

Aphorisms

The difference between Man's words and God's word is that God's word has meaning.

The proof of a word is in what it represents.

We know (2) two because it is made up of two (1) ones.

Water falls when small people appear and then again when they disappear.

The limits of language are broken by faith.

Language is the model of expression.

People pick parts they can play.

We pour concrete into our faith when we believe.

We picture God in His acts.

The gift is not gain to me until I accept it.

My time takes me away from me.

We talk about God because we can.

Everything a man wants to do have already been done. He just wants to do it all over again—just in his own way.

Jealousy is complete when pride arrives.

Anxiety leads us into the wilderness.

Gravity has to be seen in more than one picture.

Academics is the generalizations that are provable.

If language is a combination of symbols, then can any combination of symbols be a language?

If the wisdom in you be foolishness, how great is your wisdom?

Men, who hide their intellect, usually forget where.

America celebrated another victory on terror today. The Patriots beat the Jets 9–11.

Democracy has pretty legs but she is ugly.

I have neither seen nor heard of any man who was actually larger than what he thought he was.

Two lights of the same intensity differ in being separate and like Politicians, will compromise when they intersect.

People eat nothing because they have nothing to eat.

Black people, who have been taking advantage of, take advantage of themselves.

We would see success more if we weren't looking at the failures.

Actions are universal, its the issues that are particular.

People who live their lives through their music are limited by their music.

I am unsure of what I do know and sure of what I do not know.

I bump up to the edge of God but find it difficult to cross over.

Meaning wears words like clothes.

CHAPTER 9

Philosophical Poetry

Way to See

written by the writer

If mind is over matter, why does it matter? It matters because it exists. So does a relation between you and I, we—our existence, is mind over matter.

Symbols of Love

written by the writer

Where to begin?
At the moment that is now—the moment that can be proved—that can be touched.
Here is it touching me: (I inhale). Now me touching it: (I exhale).
That moment is now a part of me. I wait to experience the moment that is you.

Where will you be?
You and I will be more than the moment—you and I will be one, a we—a dis-illusion of the illusion of one, which now exist if only for the moment—but

not to us. Because we now see past language, further than the senses will allow, crossing the line of what can be perceived and what actually exists.
To us, we is one.

The Answers in her Eyes

written by the writer

He would do just about anything to experience her, to need her, to know her. She, by the way she looked at him, knew how he felt too.
It was written in what he did, what he said and what he didn't say. There were no days left that didn't bear a resemblance of the place they both hoped to find—hoped to one day be—in love.
Be in that place with me.

Resurrected Love

written by the writer

I have been here since the Genesis, right next to you, with you, carrying you and being carried. I was the it those times when life seemed like gravity, the why when memories seem to mimic autumn leaves, the who in the someone to call your own—I am with you even now.

Proof

written by the writer

I will do more than tell you, I will show you. It will be conveyed in my activity. What is to be determined will sprout from truth and remain till the next harvest. Children will paint our names in the clouds and whisper well wishes to the stars before bedtime. What will be will be us, a new, something certain and lasting. We will shutter time and impregnate the hopes of others—that they might see God too.

Truth

written by the writer

where could there be a one where a one is a sum?
the one of one functions as the one for the one.
where the one is one by one by being one.

Illusion of Truth

written by the writer

Every day there appears what some see as a new sun—a new light. A repeating pattern of newness, to them, can be, in theory, logical. As with the birth of our universe, one can expect the possibilities of the possible. This is the cornerstone to them. Without pretense or language, they are set as mere observers—set to observe their own experiences.

Contextual Straightness

written by the writer

A line has two separate and distance ends that, if imagined would lead in two separate places. What if the line was a part of the circle? Then would the line end up at the place it begun?
That same line would appear to be straight, but how could it be straight if the line exist on a sphere. It exists as a straight line only relative how it is perceived.

Words of God

written by the writer

The tools God uses are parts: what God uses is tools.

God All By Himself

written by the writer

One day as God saw me
He say to me, I will show you love
I say nothing
God say to me, I will show you love
And He gave me the thing
I say nothing
God say to me, I will show you love
And the thing loved me
But I love not the thing
God say to me, I will show you love
And I love the thing
And the thing love me
God say to me, I will show you love
And the thing love me not
But I love the thing
God say to me, I will show you love
And the thing was gone
And I love not the thing
God say to me, I will show you love
I say nothing
God say to me, I will now show you love
And I love the thing God had gave me, even though it was gone
God say to me, now I will show you love
And I love God
God say to me, now you have shown me love.

Wisdom of Love

written by the writer

love lacks no emotion
in fact, it is the antithesis of dead
rivaling only life in its beauty
sacrifices left unsaid
even change succumbs to nature
reflecting its shadow as a view
true wisdom of this world
God's love communicated through you

shadowing

written by the writer

here i am, disguised n robed.
a whore of truth, a lie untold
bear a brunt oh fool in light
hidden behind the glare of night

strum the strings that line your wall
a tall, a small, contextual
and then to whom, it must advance
a truth, is true in or out of circumstance

stand between the day and night
a symbol appears to night the light
clasped and chard a million ways
deceiving the dead, us dead men say

which they belong, a common song
a theme, a say, in which to convey
a phenomenon that's true, a truth
of fools, dependent upon of

observable proofs.

No Sooner Yet

written by the writer

simply as a simple rose
cater to a simple role
if not for an evermore
how much can there be in more
no half a sky, a all of me
have an eye, sin hypocrisy
feeling felt to no regret
feelings fail we soon forget
ladder nigh, no nectar sect
no foolish heart, no sooner yet

Verse and Prose

written by the writer

on my way 2 luv u
work do, i do
2 get 2
den next 2
d luv u
r true 2
cause dats what
we do
heaven is right here baby.

traces of u remain on me n n me …

let luv fly us 2 another day
dat our moments know

d hours of other days.

i am a cup.
wat size
i am unsure.
once i am full
den i can b measured

let us read n do without words
n let words b used unconditionally

men r a dime a dozen.
so r dimes
but u hold on 2 ones u have
precious 2u.

The Lord says to the devil back up and he listens.

A woman helps define a man
in that she shows what he is not

I say what I think. And I think what I see. I see what I think, the fallibility of
me.

Metaphorically Speaking

written by the writer

she covers me like n 8ts band
serenading parts of me wit her song
leaven me breathless, note less
wit every stroke of her tongue

Across her Face

written by the writer

She was a axiom of God—carved from the emotions of man. Her form made time envious in that he posses no power over it—he just listened to her song. Now, this woman saw this man as he saw her. He knew she saw him seeing her and felt her eyes as they ravaged every part of him—places she swore she would have. She was marking her territory and he knew it. He lay back and let her have her way till it was his turn to put his on hers and to have her say his name.

Lighthouse

written by the writer

She looks at me and quickly turns away. She didn't know but I was watching her the entire time, every since she walked into the room. Her smile left everything to the imagination, in that it was so inviting, it was like pure temptation—the kind the pastor had always warned you about. The kind of smile that had cities erected in its name, a smile that would cause other men who wanted that smile for themselves to tear down that same city. It was the enigma of her beauty—set as a sun against a world of ugliness. She was the one—the luminance that drew other lights.

Written Activity

written by the writer

He would do just about anything to experience her, to need her, to know her. She, by the way she looked at him, knew how he felt too. It was written in what he did, what he said and what he didn't say. There were no days left that didn't bear a resemblance of the place they both hoped to find—hoped to one day be—in love.

Common

written by the writer

Let nice not keep us apart but let it be summer then springtime forever. Release the experiences of the past and see not the possibilities but what is right in front of you, the now—our reality—me

Logical Atomism

written by the writer

I am that match that waits for your wick, ret te to consume you. I am the he who looks into your eyes to see you. I am the one who hears your heart even when she whispers. I am the beginning of love and the end of loneliness. I exist between a hug and a kiss, right next passion.

EVE

written by the writer

Can a woman teach a man how to humble his pride? Is she able to show him the truth is her logic? Is her hands as time that she may remake him a new? Can she hold him up and be that bone in his hip? Is a woman able to be the Father for a man that he may look up to her? Can a woman see the beauty in his pain and know that even the rocks are chiseled? What can a woman teach a man?

Crying Light

written by the writer

Every tear drop made her stronger
She sprouted wings and flew
Her world, she was the writer
Horizons under her boots

Horn Boy

written by the writer

dat boy miles
was a cool ass nigga right
we peep'd his style
but never got it right
nigga wolf—black, no spin
nigga wolf—push'n out from within
music owed dat nigga
gave life to dat nigga
spoiled us too
gave his soul for us fools
so let dat boy play
n let his soul say
dat niggas may come
till his debt repaid

Characteristics

written by the writer

What she puts on does not make her, in fact she enhances that which hangs
from her. He laid eyes on her and swore he would love no other again. She

became the it to him for which he would live. And even though she stood next to another brother who needed her as much as he did—he could see it in the way he held her, he knew after this, she would think of nothing but what would be the case, a new we. She knew like he knew she had to make her way to where she and he were to be the we.

Little Black Boys

written by the writer

Little Black boys
Love tar baths
Blackening their faces
Darkening their paths
Them little Black boys
Ain't so little no mo'
So many little black boys
So many dark souls

Still Slaves

written by the writer

Still in Jerusalem
Still on our knees
Still in the wilderness
Still crying at his feet
Still wiping away the tears
Still can see a carpenter too
Still a guest at his table
Still in need of you

Divisible to One

written by the writer

kindred time
simple paths
blessings moments
when we do have

Nigastincts

written by the writer

A nigga exist in between four walls
Four walls of which are no walls at all
Four the walls which are no walls, at all, at all
For the nigga they are real walls.

Distance Lover

written by the writer

she is curved like time
stretched out 2 appease nature
a balance 2 my counter weight
an enigma dats all mine

A Descartian Cries

written by the writer

a whited tale

oh fragile scale
a hope I feel
lamenting hell
dust d heaven
oh wisdom yell
to the heights of
a wishing well

Moses Sake

written by the writer

step by step
a steadying wall
future fray dismay
no steady wall
all
so all
so involved
future fray
no steady wall

Dead Son In Iraq

written by the writer

she shed blood 2day.
d microphone drip wet n stained
d ears of all who drank.
it washed away no pain.

Prose in Purpose:

Two to One

He whispered to her if she would mind sharing a taxi. She took him all in before she speak, her mind calculating his net worth. She looks not at his financial aptitude but she look in him: at his true value as a man—a partner, and as a one. She look hard and deep in to his eyes, then at his hands. They were no hands of a laborer: they were too small. He could build not one house with those—no hammer would have him. His hands belong at the easel or on a keyboard. She inhales as he does the same. Their quite corner of the world seems to stop and shift for a moment. Speechless they continue to communicate. What he begins to see in this woman he can't explain. And her, what she begins to feel, she desperately tries to fight. He hails a taxi. As it pulls up to the curb he opens the door for her.

She whispers back to him … closing the taxi door. She places his hand upon her heart, asking the driver to take them to her place.. Where she looked in to his eyes, she took him to her bedroom … as she made a bath for him…. she needed to take care of him, she yearned to be everything for him that night … going to heights beyond sexual, traveling as one, being one, from the moment he had her, he caressed her atom, knowing his net worth is in his brain and not in his pockets.…

That night, as he lay next to her, the moon reflecting the truth of her figure, he makes a conscious choice to love her and only her. He knows, to well, the pitfalls of a relationship—how if unnourished they wither and die. Not this flower he swore. Not if he and God had anything to say about it.

He rolls over turning on his side. He faces her now and she him; her breath beating up against his. He pushes her hair off her face. She has aged well he notes. She is flying free he contends. Why some women become butterflies while some others do not remain a mystery to him. All he knows is what is in front of him he burns for and what is in she ignites it.

Though she saw him for everything he was worth and not just what she thought was in his pockets, she somehow knew they would be safe together. He rose from the bed descending the steps of her split-level apartment. Having a seat at her white and ivory baby grand, he began to play for her. Still laying in bed, she heard the music coming up the stairs and crooned as he played. He was her Schroeder and she was his Lucy.

She rose from the bed and descended the stairs, as well, and made her way to where he was. Sitting next to him she sees his talent and feels his world meshing with hers, and this feeling is incomparable with any she has ever felt, but she knows it is real. For the first time, she speaks to him in hushed tones, her voice melodic as the piano. She tells him everything she can about herself, giving the reason that she wanted him to know her better than any other man she has ever come across and that he will be her first last kiss …

Her words to him were water; they sank in him like the sun making him the earth that rotated to her gravity. She needed nothing but to be for him to find his worth. She was him to him.

His fingers melt the white sticks one at a time and then in concert. They're decent reverberates a rich soothing scent that drives the two closer together—not in relation but in spirit.

Her words stop but not her communication. As her hips painted, her shoulders sang and her eyes composed of me a symphony.

Nothing had prepared him for this woman. Without warning she had stolen not just his heart but his mind. She had invaded his mental space, rearranged it and left it vacant every time she left. There was no turning back now, she had him and she knew it.

Conclusion

Words seem to stand separate from meaning. And if words stand separate from meaning, can any meaning be in words or is the meaning only meant by the words; tied to them? They appear to be meaningless. If words have no meaning, can they have truth in them? Can there be truth where there is no meaning? If the truth is itself and individual words are themselves, how can the words which only represent meaning and truth be the thing they are representing? It appears words have no meaning and truth in them.

If words are used by us and language, then they appear to be like tools: useful instruments in the process of working out meaning and expression: necessary only to work on language and in language. Words appear to have no meaning; meaning seems to stands behind them.

Does a word mean what it is standing in for? If it does, what does the original object in need of a stand in mean? Could the object mean itself or does it extend to a further more meaningful meaning? It appears to exist in reality and its meaning would, therefore, stand separate from its function and purpose. And if meaning corresponds to reality, then what does reality corresponds to? The meaning of reality seems to be in the position and relevance of the objects in that reality. They appear to all have in common the condition of relations. Even if we attempted to create a different reality, it would have in common with this one; a relation of some sort. Even matter has anti-matter as a counterpart as well as particles and anti-particles co-exist.

If meaning is tied to reality, where are words in reality? If the written word is words in reality, did words exist in reality before they were written down? If the words existed before they were written down, then how can the meaning be that which came after that which already existed? Or if the word didn't exist, how can meaning be given to that which is not in reality?

It would appear that either the word or the object for which the word stands in for has to have meaning. It appears to be one or the other. If one is pointing to the other, then the one who is pointing would appear to be pointing to the one with the meaning: the word to reality.

Should we ask what the word is representing instead of asking what the meaning of a word is? When we ask about meaning, should we be asking about reality? Is meaning tangible or can the unobservable have meaning? It appears things exist that aren't observable (yet). Are ideas or thoughts those things that exist that aren't observable? If I imagine a time-machine does that make the time-machine real or just the idea of the time-machine? Does it exist independent of anyone thinking about it or before I thought about it?

A machine that travels across time is an idea that respects the concept of restraints on time. The concept of traveling opposed to those restraints stands behind the previous sentence as a relation to expose the true idea. This concept of loosening time seems to exist because of the concept of constraints of time. The idea of restraint on time seems to suggest the conceptualized antithesis of restraint; loose. Therefore, we can conclude that with time came time travel. Yet time is unobservable. Since we can only see the effects of time, so then we can only see the effect of time travel.

Time does appear to have meaning, yet appearances can deceive. If reality has meaning, then is it the objects that time affects that have the meaning that is being observed or time itself?

Understand what is being expressed:

Language is language.
What language is is a way of reading.
What you read will determine the language.
Questions do not relate to reality they relate to interpretation.
Mans language is substance-less, it contains facts but not truth or conveyed meaning; even this sentence.

Language portrays understanding not reality.
Words are empty shells waiting to be filled by us.
Meaning is a tool: a word used in and by language; represents one of the three.
Truth is separate from fact: a sentence may be a fact but never the truth.
We only express interpretations of the truth in language, not the truth itself.
Words clothed themselves in knock offs of the truth.
We only use language to get to understanding.
What we hope to understand is not the language.
We use language to express what we understand.
In our language, it is not what we understand itself that is being conveyed, but our interpretation of what we understand; the idea or concept.
Even though we use language to acquire understanding, we understand separate from language.
We agree to language to help us get to understanding.
I agree within the process to get to understanding.
I compare/contrast to get to agreement within the process to get to understanding.
What I compare/contrast is X vs. X-1 to get to agreement within the process to get to understanding.

So what I am saying is these processes of compare/contrast and agreement, act as the foundation to understanding then on to meaning. Where that data is retrieved will only determine the quality of the understanding (in a sense). It will reference only a view of the reality it is attempting to portray.

But these "basic functions" act as the wheels of our minds, stimulating other functions that aid in the crafting and shaping of our beliefs, building ladders to our understandings, and wholly separate from language if need be. Our language is merely the wrench of our minds.

A note worthy point is to answer the question of total agreement. It, total universal agreement, is not premised as the process of knowledge, only that agreement must exist as a basic component for knowledge itself to exist.

Within the process of understanding, it appears there has to be agreement. What fact is there in reality is there that qualifies black as a fact? No other presuppositions exist for that fact except agreement in language. In essence, the color black is recognized as a fact within language because we have agreed upon that very fact. It is not a truth. As reference, the color black as we know it is not black (as a fact) in Portugal. The word "preto" represents the fact there. If agreement is not within the process of knowing, then we both have no facts.

I guess what I am pointing out is that language props up facts and that agreement is a crutch to language. We can communicate when we have agreed upon a few basic things like structure, parts, definitions, etc …

There too, knowledge is not dependent upon facts. Though it is significant in many instances, it is not totally necessary. Even though I can only believe what I can understand or what I believe I understand, what I can believe may exist separate from any known fact; which may be seen from many vantage points.

What I am theorizing is that we acquire knowledge without language and through language. We acquire knowledge without language by comparing and contrasting till agreement is reached. Agreement may be reached without language even as subtle as a crying baby after receiving a bottle stops crying. The baby who is without language begins to compare and contrast conditions, experiences, multiple stimuli, all in attempts to gain some understanding: in which he may be unaware he is attempting. It is the agreement upon the satisfying of certain condition that makes the connection for him or her. Certain understandings may be realized. It's only then can language be learned. The baby has to be able to associate reality to the words it is attempting to learn. It would appear that understanding the reality must precede associating meaning of words to that reality.

So then, once we have reached this annex of realization, we use language as stand-ins within the process of understanding to, either further cement our own understanding or to express that understanding.

Language then is a tool: a tool to be used to express and understand. And as its nature, presupposes some basic requirements such as agreement and comparing/contrast. With that, the essence of how we determine realization determines how we realize language. It is the language that presupposes reality.

Theories of Language

"All language is readable even if it is unreadable."

What I mean by this is that words are not the language. Words are used by the language the way gravity used the apple for Newton. Language like gravity grabs a hold of the apple and takes it through its motions, motions we can observe, reason and ascertain meaning from—and in much the same manner as Newton too. Babies, for instance, grasp at understanding, clawing through errors of misjudgment, stumbling over the misguided interpretations of meaning till understanding is finally reached. Once that first understanding is accomplished, the baby can now move on to more complex and richer understandings; understandings that provide meaning.

What we contend to be language most times is confused by it parts. When we hear or read certain words we immediately assume it to be a certain language. We hear words spoken or see words written in the English format and automatically assume it to be part of the structure and code of English; we then set about trying to decipher and decode the cryptic message. Ebonics should have been lesson enough for most of us, yet skeptics remain. The first step in deciphering or decoding any message is to determine who it is from and in what language is the message being sent. It would seem fantastically odd to try to read something before determining what language it was in.

And lastly, where we see no language often times, language may exist. For instance: A tree has roots that are connected to the soil, which is connected to the nutrients in the soil, which is connected to other things and so on. The tree has components such as branches, leaves, bugs, all vital parts in its existence.

Although the tree appears to be a living organism capable of some form of reproducing, it still is dependent on other factors in order to ascertain its true purpose. Each thing has its own properties, hard, soft, large, green, brown; all adding to the vitality of the tree. Now take a look at language. It, too, has a similar structure: propositions, sentences, paragraphs, and books, each built on top of or in connection with or in connection to all the other parts. All designed and dependent upon one another, so the force and strength of the "all" is adding to its true weight as a statement. The existence of the tree makes a statement much like the sentence or paragraph. They all tell a story, express a thought, reveal a truth or in the trees case, testify to the death, burial and resurrection of Jesus Christ. These expressions are to be interpreted by those who are trying to determine what is being said.

"Languages stand shoulder to shoulder."

What I am referring to is the phenomenon like Ebonics. We speak different languages, standing on different shoulders all the time. When we speak using the parts of a language, we speak from its pulpit. That pulpit determines how our message will be received; its context. Ebonics and English stand so close to one another that we confuse the shoulders of the one whom the speaker is standing. This confusion of pulpits is the basis for most misunderstandings. The confusion comes in when you try to interpret the parts of the language assuming the speaker is from a particular shoulder when he or she may be a few shoulders down. Languages evolve like fungus. They infiltrate and attach themselves to similar species of languages and begin to mimic their counterparts while slipping slight little nuances into the DNA of the new being. What is created is a similar but, be it, a different language, full bodied and shouldered. This phenomenon is more common than we think.

"There is no "No" language."

Everything appears to speak to something. This can be seen in its most classical form in David Hume's theory of causality or under Newton's third law of motion. With this understanding, we try to read nature in all of its splendor; piggybacking ideas and concepts with one another, hoping to achieve a level of understanding of the unknown without using one of mans most basic concepts for understanding. We limit ourselves by trying to understand before we learn to read; thinking language comes in one form is a mistake made by us all at one point or another. But experience seems to be a good teacher, except Hume. We learn to read traffic, read faces, expression and even attitudes when we read reality.

"Everything that can be done with language can be done without language."

If words are the parts of language and language is only the structure I use to communicate, then does what I communicate exist before I attempt to communicate it? Am I using language before that? Do I need language to communicate with myself? How do babies learn if they have no language? What I am saying is that we understand without language. We understand what we think there is to know. Let's say for instance we see a car turned upside down and its passengers lay out in the street. What happens is we observe and compare the objects in reality. We attempt to recognize the phenomenon. Immediately the positions of the objects begin to reflect a certain truth we think we realize; we know. The objects and the activity take on names as well as the phenomenon itself. What happens then is we take and use language within ourselves for a better understanding (repeating sentences or reworking sentences to ourselves to better clarify the reality) and for others. So when we go to express that reality, it will be best portrayed using the truest portrayal of that reality. Understanding is contrasting and comparing in a sense. We compare and contrast in the visual, using sound, using the sensation of touch: we also use what we already know, experiential data, and other theories all to determine distinct variations we recognize as meanings. We use all our senses, experience, science; any data that is available to determine what there is to know.

"Truth about language is that language has no truth in it except when the truth is the language."

Remembering we only use language and its parts to communicate those expressions of reality, either to ourselves or to each other, we, with the help of language, hijack the truth of reality and masquerade language as it. We speak or express our understanding not truth itself. Even if we see objects or the world objectively and seek to express that reality objectively, the language we use to express that objectiveness can in no way have that actual objectiveness it is expressing in it. That would appear to contradict reality. For instance, could our words or our expressions contain the actual objects or the reality in which we are attempting to express about the car and its occupants? Are my sentences and propositions the actual objects or representations of the activity, objects or phenomenon? Even if I attempt to use the objects themselves to express a thought, I still am not since it is the objects themselves that is doing the speaking not me. What this seems to suggest is that language is language and not the thing or things in which is trying to express. Therefore, our language would have no truth in it unless that language is reality, it can not be the thing it is expressing.

"Language portrays understanding not reality."

Once a language is learned, it does not become the de facto language of our minds. We only use language as the tool to cement the understanding. We may have to say a sentence over to ourselves a few times, in some instances, in order for the concrete to harden in our understanding or to truly get what is being meant. If it were the words themselves we were trying to understand, then one might conclude it's the language or its parts that is the obstacle. But, in fact, it appears I am trying to understanding the meanings of the propositions in a way that is separate from the words or the language. I truly am trying to understand the meaning behind the words: what the words are referring or pointing to. It appears I do not need language to learn or to understand, I only use language as an easel to paint that understanding.

The final conclusion of this book is the activity it produces. This activity stands as the proof—proof that the idea that words have no meaning and are to be used like wrenches, tools, is wisdom. The idea that language presupposes reality and that our language is comprised of empty shells void of truth and any conveyed meaning is meaningful itself. This book stands as wisdom because it can has the capacity to produce better and more developed thinking; which ultimately will lead to a more, better and developed thinking being.

To the reader, the hope is that no longer will you see the symbol as chained down to rudimentary meanings; weighting only so much. Words, we hope will become viewed as screwdrivers, bolts, nuts, hammers: all necessary configurations of form and structure we pull out of our mental toolboxes and set up against that which we hope to convey or to understand.

After experiencing this book, language, will appear to begin to stand out more eloquently, in that the objects and the activity in reality will begin to speak for themselves; they're voices can now be heard over ours. In fact, one may begin to notice new languages and new words of that language expressing new facts about the same truth. Now, these languages and words can be seen in their own form, their own languages and in the structure of their original expression. And finally, yet finally, the chains that once held firm us and the word will forever be broken that we might all see God more clearly in his son, Jesus Christ.

Index

978-0-595-48644-1
0-595-48644-4